Prentice Hall

Student-Centered
Science Activities
for the
Midwest

Prentice Hall
Upper Saddle River, New Jersey
Needham, Massachusetts

Prentice Hall
Student-Centered Science Activities for the Midwest

Contributing Writers

Bill Badders
Science Teacher
Joseph F. Landis Elementary School
Cleveland, Ohio

E. John De Waard
Science Writer
Vernon Hills, Illinois

Margaret Flack
Science Teacher
Jasper Middle School
Jasper, Indiana

Karen Henman
Science Teacher
Woodrow Wilson Middle School
Terre Haute, Indiana

Gregory Sloan
Science Teacher
Otter Creek Middle School
Terre Haute, Indiana

Bruce A. Starek
Science Teacher
Barker Middle School
Michigan City, Indiana

ISBN 0-13-435869-4

3 4 5 6 7 8 9 10   02 01 00 99

PRENTICE HALL

CONTENTS

INTRODUCTION

The *Student-Centered Science Activities for the Midwest* book contains 12 activities that have been specifically written for students in the midwestern states. In most cases, these activities were written by middle-school teachers who teach in the Midwest.

Activities

The 12 region-specific activities will not only help students understand some of the major concepts involved in earth, life, and physical science, but also give students an opportunity to see the relevance of science in their own region. Of the 12 region-specific activities, four are geared to earth science, four to life science, and four to physical science.

Answer Key

The Answer Key contains answers to all the Observations and Analyze and Conclude segments of each activity. Also found in the Answer Key are Teacher Notes that offer special tips or suggestions for preparing materials or for helping students perform the activities.

Correlation to Prentice Hall Science Programs

Finally, the Correlation to *Prentice Hall Earth Science, Prentice Hall Life Science, Prentice Hall Physical Science, Prentice Hall Science Explorer,* and *Prentice Hall Science* lists the sections of these books to which each student-centered activity corresponds.

Name _____ Class_____ Date _____

Activity 1 **Locating the Epicenter of an Earthquake**

Background Information

When an earthquake occurs, vibrations are sent out in all directions from the earthquake's epicenter. These vibrations are recorded by machines called seismographs. Scientists determine the location of the epicenter of an earthquake by comparing data from seismographs in at least three locations. The first vibration detected by the seismograph is known as the primary, or P, wave. P waves travel at a speed of 6 kilometers per second. Like sound waves, P waves vibrate, causing rock particles to move back and forth in the same direction that the wave is traveling. Moving at half the speed of a P wave (3 km/sec), the secondary, or S, wave is the next wave to reach the seismograph. S waves cause the rocks to vibrate at right angles to the direction the wave is traveling. L waves are the slowest waves and cause most of the damage during an earthquake.

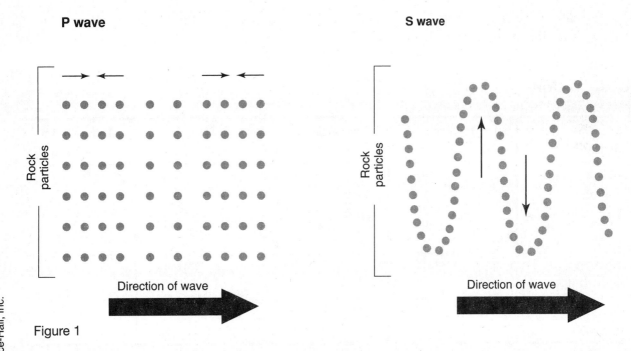

Figure 1

Problem

How can you locate the epicenter of an earthquake using four different seismograph stations?

Materials (per group of students)

    calculator
    compass
    metric ruler
    pencil
    map of the United States with key in kilometers

Procedure

1. Using the arrival times of the P waves given in the Data Table and the speed at which P waves travel, calculate the distance of each seismograph station from the epicenter. Record your results in the appropriate places in the Data Table.

2. Using the arrival times of the S waves given in the Data Table and the speed at which S waves travel, again calculate the distance of each seismograph station from the epicenter. Record your results in the appropriate places in the Data Table.

3. Compare the results you obtained in Steps 1 and 2. If your results for Step 1 are not the same as your results for Step 2, repeat Steps 1 and 2.

4. Using the map key, set the compass to the distance from the epicenter you calculated for Indianapolis, Indiana. Use the compass to draw a circle on the map with Indianapolis at the center of the circle. Repeat this procedure for Wichita, Kansas; Bismarck, North Dakota; and Madison, Wisconsin.

5. Locate the epicenter of the earthquake. The epicenter will be the point at which all four of the circles meet.

Observations

DATA TABLE

Location	P wave arrival time	Distance to epicenter	S wave arrival time	Distance to epicenter
Indianapolis, Indiana	1 min., 23 sec.		2 min., 46 sec.	
Wichita, Kansas	1 min., 51 sec.		3 min., 42 sec.	
Bismarck, North Dakota	4 min., 18 sec.		8 min., 36 sec.	
Madison, Wisconsin	2 min., 13 sec.		4 min., 26 sec.	

Analyze and Conclude

1. Compare the length of time it takes for a P wave and an S wave to reach a seismograph station.

_____

_____

_____

_____

_____

_____

_____

2. The earthquake you studied in the procedure is the New Madrid, Missouri, earthquake of 1811 and 1812. Where is the epicenter of the New Madrid earthquake?

_____

_____

_____

3. Why do seismologists need information from at least three different seismograph stations to determine the location of an earthquake?

_____

_____

_____

_____

_____

_____

_____

4. The New Madrid fault system starts at Cairo, Illinois, and extends through New Madrid, Missouri, and Caruthersville, Missouri, down through Blythsville, Arkansas, and finally to Marked Tree, Arkansas. Along the way, the fault also reaches into Kentucky near Fulton, and into Tennessee near Reelfoot Lake. Use this description and a detailed atlas to sketch the New Madrid fault on the map. Approximately how long is the New Madrid fault?

_____

_____

_____

_____

_____

Activity 2 Communicating About the Weather

Background Information

Meteorologists display information about the weather in weather maps. The weather maps that appear in weather reports on television and in newspapers combine weather data from observation stations across the country. These observation stations provide local weather information to the National Weather Service in the form of station models. A station model contains a variety of different symbols. Each symbol provides a different piece of information about the weather in a given location. The symbols represent such weather factors as wind speed and direction, cloud cover, and precipitation.

Problem

How can you use a station model to communicate the weather?

Materials (per group)

pencil
paper
weather report from a newspaper

Procedure

1. Study the sample station model in Figure 1 on page 5. Fill in the weather information for the station model in the appropriate place in the Data Table.

2. Using the information in the weather report assigned to your group, create a station model. You might have to hypothesize about some of the weather factors, such as the type of clouds.

3. In the Data Table, record the date and location for the station model you created. Then fill in the weather information for your station model in the Data Table.

4. Have one member of your group draw the station model on the board along with the station models from the other groups. The station models should appear in order according to the date from which the weather data for each model was taken.

5. Write a weather report based on the information in the station model you created. Have one member of your group read the weather report to the class.

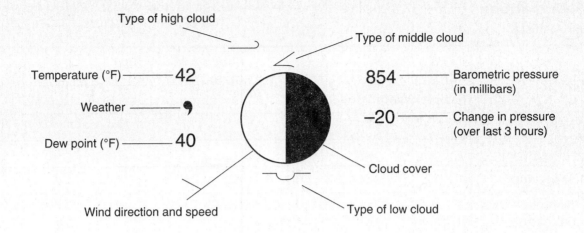

Type of high cloud

Type of middle cloud

Temperature (°F) —— 42

854 —— Barometric pressure (in millibars)

Weather —— ❟

−20 —— Change in pressure (over last 3 hours)

Dew point (°F) —— 40

Cloud cover

Wind direction and speed

Type of low cloud

Cloud cover	Symbol
0%	◯
10%	◐
20%–30%	◕
50%	◑
60%	◑
70%–80%	◕
90%	◕
100%	●

High clouds	Symbol
cirrus	⌐
cirrostratus	2
cirrocumulus	⌁

Middle clouds	Symbol
altostratus	∠
nimbostratus	⫫
altocumulus	⌣

Low clouds	Symbol
cumulus	⌓
stratocumulus	⌣
stratus	—
cumulonimbus	⎏

Weather	Symbol
fog	≡
shower	▽
thunderstorm	⌐↘
ice pellets	△
hail	⬦
freezing rain	•↷•
freezing drizzle	↷↶
drizzle	❟
rain	•
snow	✳
hurricane	⸨

Wind speed (1 knot = 1.85 km/h)	Symbol
0 (calm)	◯
1–2 knots	╱
3–7 knots	⤙
8–12 knots	⌄
13–17 knots	⤸
18–22 knots	⤻
23–27 knots	⤼
48–52 knots	⧖

© Prentice-Hall, Inc.

Figure 1

Observations

DATA TABLE

	Sample Station Model	Station Model for Date _____ Location _____
Wind speed		
Wind direction		
Temperature		
Dew point temperature		
Barometric pressure		
Change in pressure		
Cloud cover		
Precipitation		
Cloud types		

Analyze and Conclude

1. Observe all of your classmates' station models. Which weather factors stayed nearly the same during the five-day period you studied? Which weather factors changed?

   _____

   _____

   _____

2. What is the only symbol on the station models that appears in a different location on different days?

   _____

   _____

3. Did you have to hypothesize about any of the weather factors in your station model? If so, which factor was it and how did you come up with your hypothesis?

   _____

   _____

   _____

4. Do the station models show a relationship between barometric pressure and the presence of clouds? If so, what is the relationship?

_____

_____

_____

5. Do the station models show a relationship between barometric pressure and the presence of precipitation? If so, what is the relationship?

_____

_____

_____

6. Why do you think meteorologists use station models?

_____

_____

_____

7. Based on the station models prepared by your classmates and your knowledge of weather patterns, predict the weather for the day after the five-day period you studied.

_____

_____

_____

8. How does your group's report compare with that of the National Weather Service for the day after the five-day period you studied? (If you have access to the Internet, log on to the National Oceanic and Atmospheric Administration Web site at http://www.noaa.gov/ to find out if your local weather prediction was correct.)

_____

_____

_____

Activity 3 **Using a Contour Map to Create a Landform**

Background Information

Ancient glaciers were responsible for shaping much of the Earth, including the midwestern United States. Parts of the midwest that were covered by glaciers are made up of flat, fertile plains, with a rolling landscape and many ponds and lakes. One type of landform that was made by ancient glaciers and is found in the Midwest is a drumlin. A drumlin is an oval-shaped mound of rocks and soil deposited directly by a glacier. Most drumlins have one steep end and one end with a gentle slope. The steep end of a drumlin faces the direction from which the glacier came.

One of the tools scientists use to study the landscape and its history is contour maps. Contour maps are also called topographic maps. The high and low elevations created by mountains, hills, and valleys cannot be observed on a typical map. Contour maps show differences in elevation, or height above sea level, and outline the shapes, or contours, of the landscape using isolines. An isoline connects the points on a map that have the same elevation. The contour interval is the difference in elevation between one contour line and the next.

Problem

How can you use a contour map to create a landform?

Materials (per group)

transparent plastic box with lid
nonpermanent marking pen
enlarged photocopy of regional contour map
modeling clay
meter ruler

Procedure

1. Using a nonpermanent marking pen, trace the enlarged contour map provided by your teacher onto the box lid.

2. Using the marking pen and a ruler, place a centimeter scale on the side of the transparent box. Mark the bottom of the box as 0 cm and continue until you reach the top of the box.

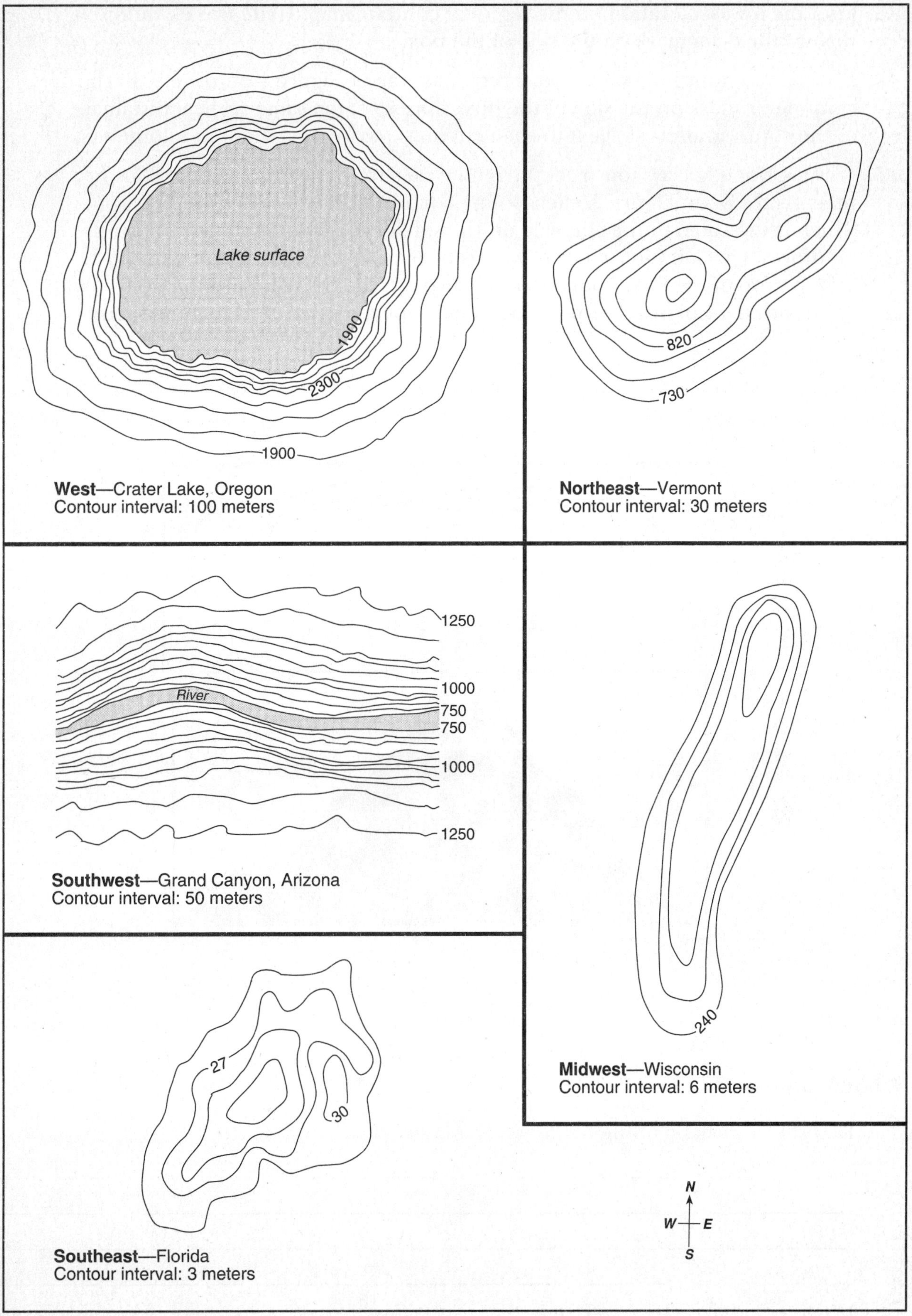
Lake surface
1900
2300
1900
West—Crater Lake, Oregon
Contour interval: 100 meters
820
730
Northeast—Vermont
Contour interval: 30 meters
1250
River
1000
750
750
1000
1250
Southwest—Grand Canyon, Arizona
Contour interval: 50 meters
240
Midwest—Wisconsin
Contour interval: 6 meters
27
30
Southeast—Florida
Contour interval: 3 meters
N
W
E
S

Figure 1

3. Find the lowest elevation on the regional contour map. Write this elevation next to the 0-cm mark on the side of the box.

4. Find the contour interval for your regional map in Figure 1 on page 9. Each centimeter mark on the side of the box represents the same vertical distance as the contour interval. Next to each cm mark, write the height in kilometers.

5. Using modeling clay, construct the landform shown in your regional contour map. As shown in Figure 2, each isoline corresponds to a different elevation, which is indicated in the cm scale on the side of the box. As you construct the landform, check it for accuracy. Do this by placing the lid with the contour map on top of the box. Looking down through the lid, compare the land form with the isolines shown on the map. Repeat this procedure as needed.

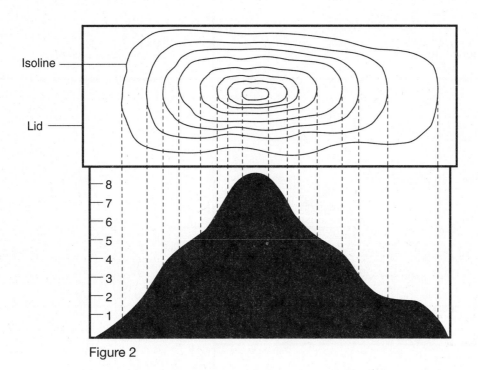

Figure 2

Observations

1. Describe the shape of the landform you created.

_____

_____

_____

_____

_____

2. How many meters above sea level is the base of the landform?

_____

3. What is the contour interval of the contour map you used to create the landform?

_____

Analyze and Conclude

1. Does the landform you constructed fit the description of a drumlin? Explain your answer.

_____

_____

_____

_____

_____

_____

2. From which direction did the glacier that made the drumlin come?

_____

_____

3. Compare the contour map for the Midwest with the contour map for the Northeast. Do you think the hill in the map for the Northeast is a drumlin also? Explain your answer.

_____

_____

_____

_____

_____

_____

4. Describe the landscape in the area where you live. Are there drumlins in your area?

_____

_____

_____

_____

_____

_____

_____

_____

_____

Activity 4 **Observing Erosion and Deposition**

Background Information

Erosion is the removal of soil by the action of wind, water, gravity, glaciers, and waves. When erosion occurs, rocks and soil are moved from one place to another, changing the landscape. The placement of soil in a new location is called deposition. The moving water in rivers, creeks, and streams is a major cause of erosion. Because the Midwest has an abundant number of rivers, creeks, and streams, its landscape is constantly being transformed by erosion and deposition.

Problem

What are some of the factors that affect erosion and deposition?

Materials (per group)

paper cup	metric ruler
pencil	soil
drinking straw	books
scissors	water
modeling clay	paper towels
large sheet of cardboard	rocks

Procedure

1. Using a pencil, make a hole in a paper cup close to the bottom.

2. Cut the straw in half with scissors and insert one of the halves in the hole in the cup. **CAUTION:** *Be careful when using sharp instruments.*

3. Use modeling clay to form a seal around the straw. Make sure the straw and clay fill the hole tightly.

4. Using a metric ruler, measure the length of the cardboard in centimeters. Record this information in the Data Table.

5. Place the cardboard on the ground and put a thin layer of soil over the entire square of cardboard.

6. Raise one end of the cardboard about 5 cm from the ground by placing books under the raised end.

7. Place the cup in the middle of the raised end of the cardboard so that the straw is pointing downhill. See Figure 1 on page 13.

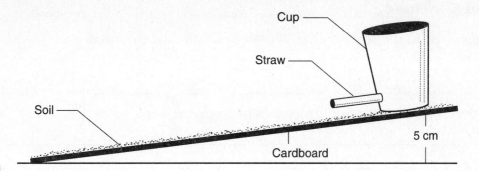

Cup

Straw

Soil

5 cm

Cardboard

Figure 1

8. Place your finger over the opening of the straw as your partner fills the cup with water.

9. Remove your finger. Observe what happens to the water and the soil. Record your observations in the Data Table.

10. Clean the cardboard with paper towels and cover it with soil again.

11. Now raise the end of the board about 15 cm from the ground and repeat Steps 7 through 10.

12. Lower the end of the cardboard to 5 cm from the ground. Repeat Steps 7 through 10 again, but this time place a small rock on the cardboard directly in front of the straw. Record your observations about how water moves around the rock in the Data Table.

13. Keeping the end of the cardboard 5 cm from the ground, repeat Steps 7 through 10 a third time, but this time place a pile of several small rocks or one large rock on the cardboard directly in front of the straw. Again, record your observations about how water moves around the rocks in the Data Table.

14. The slope, or slant, of a stream is equal to the vertical drop divided by the horizontal distance traveled. Using the length of the cardboard and the height it is raised, calculate the slope of the "stream" in each part of the procedure. Record your calculations in the Data Table.

Observations

DATA TABLE

Length of cardboard _____

Elevation of Cardboard	Slope	Quantity of rocks	Observations
5 cm		None	
15 cm		None	
5 cm		One small	
5 cm		Several small (or one large)	

© Prentice-Hall, Inc.

Analyze and Conclude

1. What happened to the soil particles that were carried by the stream?

   _____

   _____

2. Does water erosion create smooth curves or sharp angles?

   _____

   _____

3. What effect did raising the elevation of the cardboard have on the speed of the water?

   _____

   _____

4. What effect did the speed of the water have on the erosion of the soil and the path of the stream?

   _____

   _____

5. What is the relationship between the slope of a stream and the rate of erosion?

   _____

   _____

6. Compare the movement of the water with one rock, and then several rocks, in front of the straw. Explain any differences in movement.

   _____

   _____

7. How do boulders in the bed of a river affect the motion of the water?

   _____

   _____

8. In general, the landscape of the Midwest has few slopes. Describe erosion in the Midwest compared to erosion in mountainous regions such as the West.

   _____

   _____

   _____

Activity 1 **Investigating Ecological Succession**

Background Information

Change is a natural part of life in any ecological community. Animals may move to a new location, or a disease may wipe them out. Extreme changes in weather or a natural disaster may reduce the number of some plants or animals, yet enable other plants or animals to survive.

Whenever change occurs in a community, some habitats may be destroyed, while new ones are created. For example, a forest fire may eliminate the habitat of birds. In addition to fires, other natural disasters such as floods, earthquakes, and volcanic eruptions can destroy or change communities. Over time, new communities of organisms may gradually replace existing ones in a process called ecological succession. See Figure 1.

Figure 1

The first organisms to occupy a new ecological community are called pioneer organisms. Some pioneer organisms are small plants. These plants create a layer of soil in which larger plants can grow. As the plants become taller, they provide shade. The shade partially blocks the sunlight, causing some plants to die. Dead plants add humus to the soil. Humus is decaying material that is necessary for plant growth. The greater the amount of humus in the soil, the taller the plants can grow. And as the dominant plants in an area change, so do the dominant animals.

When the plants and animals that make up a community change, the community develops into a different type of community, with different plants and animals. This process repeats itself until a stable community eventually forms. The stable community is called a climax community. The time it takes for succession to form a climax community can range from several decades to thousands of years.

Problem

How does ecological succession occur in a community?

Materials (per pair of students)

4 stacks of game cards   number cubes
game board   2 paper clips or other small objects

Procedure

1. Spread out the game board on a flat surface. Next to the game board, place the stacks of game cards with the community names face up.

2. Place a paper clip or other small object on any box on the game board. This object will be your marker as you play.

3. Roll one number cube. Read the number on the cube and move your marker the same number of squares.

4. Notice the color of the square on which you landed. Choose a card that is the same color as the square. Place the card on the square so that the side with the picture of a plant or animal is face up. Note the community to which the plant or animal belongs. Write the name of the plant or animal in the appropriate place in the Data Table.

5. Have your partner follow steps 2 through 4.

6. Repeat steps 2 through 5 until every square on the game board contains a picture of a plant or animal.

Observations

DATA TABLE

Organisms	Lake Michigan Sand-Dune Communities			
	Open beach	Fore-dune cottonwood	Jack pine	Oak forest
Plants				
Animals				

Analyze and Conclude

1. Which community in the Lake Michigan sand dunes has the most pioneer plants? How do the pioneer plants affect the community?

_____

_____

2. Compare the sizes of the plants in the open-beach community with those in the oak-forest community. Explain any differences in plant size.

_____

_____

3. Which community has mammals? Why do you think this community has mammals while the others do not?

_____

_____

4. The open-beach community along Lake Michigan receives more direct sunlight than the oak-forest community. How do you think differences in the amount of light affect living things in these communities?

_____

_____

5. The four communities along the shores of Lake Michigan have been developing for 8000 years. Which community was the first to form? Which of the four communities you studied in this activity was the last to form?

_____

6. Describe a natural event that could disturb the communities of the Lake Michigan sand dunes. How might the event affect the process of ecological succession?

_____

_____

_____

7. Describe the effects of humans on ecological succession.

_____

_____

_____

8. Observe an area close to your school, such as woods, a vacant lot, or the bottom of a fence. Describe the stages of ecological succession you think have taken place in the area.

_____

_____

_____

9. The climax community for the Lake Michigan sand dunes area is a beech-maple forest. How do you think the plants in this community compare to those in the oak-forest community?

_____

_____

_____

Activity 2 **Classifying Leaves**

Background Information

Classification keys are tools for the identification of plants and animals. Classification keys may also be called dichotomous keys. The word dichotomous comes from the word dichotomy, which means "two opposite parts or categories." A dichotomous key provides two statements about some trait of an organism. Each statement is the opposite of the other. By choosing the statement that best describes the organism, the user is led to another pair of opposite statements. The user continues to choose between statements, and eventually is led to the classification of the unknown organism.

A branching chart is a method of showing the division of organisms by a dichotomous key. Figure 1 shows a branching chart for the set of shapes above it. First the shapes are divided into two groups according to their color, white or black. Another characteristic further divides the black objects into two groups, and another divides the white objects into two groups. The black objects are divided into those that have one or more straight edges and those that have no straight edges. The white objects are separated according to whether they are square or round. The objects are divided again and again until each one is separately categorized.

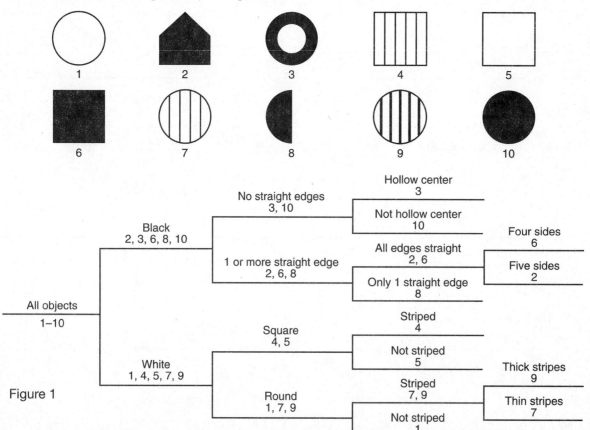

Figure 1

Problem

How can you classify leaves using a dichotomous key?

Procedure

1. Study Figure 2, which shows the leaves of the state trees of a number of mid-western states. Notice the different characteristics in the shapes of the leaves. Choose a characteristic to separate the leaves into two groups.

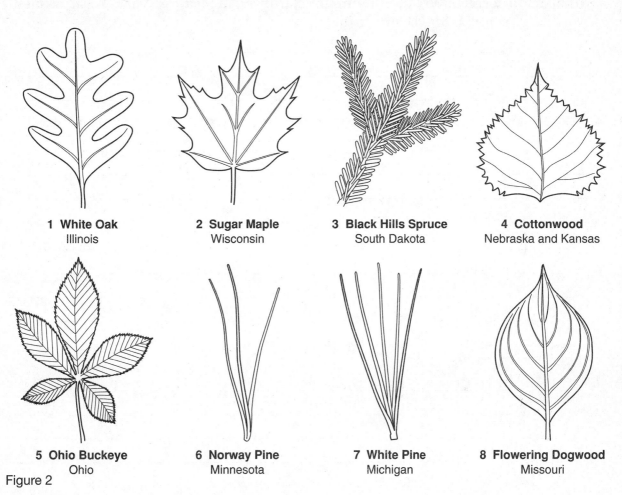

1 White Oak
Illinois

2 Sugar Maple
Wisconsin

3 Black Hills Spruce
South Dakota

4 Cottonwood
Nebraska and Kansas

5 Ohio Buckeye
Ohio

6 Norway Pine
Minnesota

7 White Pine
Michigan

8 Flowering Dogwood
Missouri

Figure 2

2. On a separate sheet of paper, make a chart similar to the one shown in Figure 1 to show how you divided the leaves.

3. Choose a characteristic to divide each subgroup you created into further subgroups. Continue this procedure until each leaf has a separate category. Use Figure 1 as a model for creating your branching chart.

4. Have another student use your chart to see if she or he can identify each leaf.

Observations

Include your leaf classification key.

Analyze and Conclude

1. Is your classification system different from your classmates'? Why might this be possible?

_____

_____

_____

2. What characteristics were most useful for classifying the leaves? What characteristics would not be useful for classifying them?

_____

_____

_____

3. Why should you avoid terms like large and small when describing organisms?

_____

_____

_____

4. How does classification help you to understand organisms better?

_____

_____

_____

_____

5. Suggest two ways in which you could identify trees during winter when they have no leaves.

_____

_____

_____

_____

6. Collect leaves from a wooded area near your home or school. Try to classify them using the branching chart you created. Do they fit into your chart? Explain why or why not.

_____

_____

_____

Activity 3 **Observing the Effects of Acid Rain**

Background Information

The main source of air pollution is the burning of fossil fuels. Motor vehicles, power plants, and factories burn fossil fuels to produce energy. When fossil fuels are burned, they release sulfur dioxides and nitrogen oxides into the air. In the clouds, these gases react with water vapor, forming sulfuric acid and nitric acid. These strong acids fall to Earth as acid rain. Acid rain is the popular term for acid precipitation, which includes rain, snow, sleet, and fog.

Because more-populated areas, such as large cities, have more vehicles and factories, they produce more acid rain than less-populated areas. Weather patterns such as wind currents move acidic clouds away from areas where the acids are produced to other areas. Because acid rain can take many hours to several days to form, the atmosphere often carries it great distances before it falls to the Earth.

Scientists use the pH scale to measure the acidity of substances. The lower the pH, the more acidic the substance is. See Figure 1.

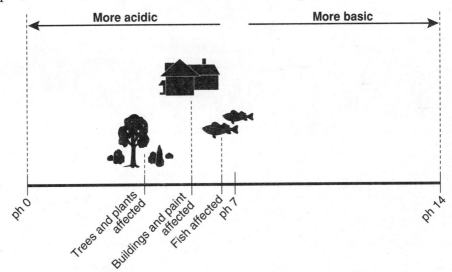

Figure 1

The pH of normal rainwater is 5.6. If rainwater has a pH lower than 5.6, it is considered acid rain. Some acid rain may soak into soil, lowering the pH of the soil. If the soil contains a buffer, however, the pH of the soil will not be changed. A buffer resists changes in pH by neutralizing some or all of the acid in the soil. Lime is a buffer that is often used to neutralize acid in soil.

Even though soil may be protected from acid rain by buffers, trees in the same area can be harmed by acid fog, which is even more damaging to trees than acid rain. When leaves are bathed in acid fog, their protective waxy coating wears off. Soon brown spots develop on the leaves. These spots prevent leaves from capturing sunlight in order to perform photosynthesis, the process by which green plants produce food. If the leaves cannot produce enough food energy for the trees, they become weak and unhealthy and are less able to defend themselves against disease and insects.

Problem

How does pollution from large cities affect national forests?

Materials (per student)

metric ruler   pencil

Procedure

Use the Background Information and the map to answer the questions in Observations and Analyze and Conclude.

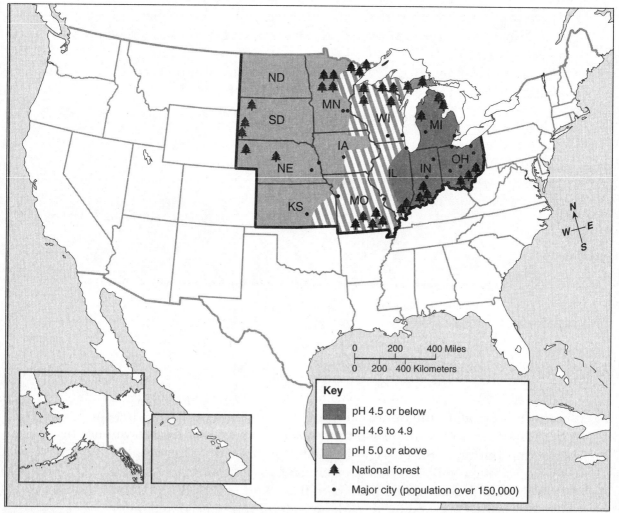

Figure 2

Observations

1. Which state has a higher pH level of the soil—Ohio or North Dakota? Which of these two states has a higher acid level?

   _____

2. What is the pH level at which trees and plants are affected?

   _____

3. Which states have national forests in areas where the pH is 5.0 or higher? Where the pH is 4.6 to 4.9?

   _____

   _____

4. Which states have national forests in areas where the pH is 4.5 or lower?

   _____

Analyze and Conclude

1. Why do the states you listed in Observations question 4 have the lowest pH?

   _____

   _____

2. Which states have national forests that are least in danger of being damaged by acid rain?

   _____

3. Do any midwestern states have a pH low enough to damage trees and plants? If not, do you think this could change? Explain your answer.

   _____

   _____

4. Compare the pH level in your area with the pH in the rest of the Midwest. Is your area affected by pollution from major cities? Explain your answer.

   _____

   _____

   _____

5. Why do you think acid fog is more damaging to trees than acid rain is?

   _____

   _____

6. Forests are beneficial to life in many different ways. Log on to the United States Environmental Protection Agency Web site at http://www.epa.gov/ acidrain/student/todo.html to find out how forests can be protected from acid rain. On a separate sheet of paper, make a list of some of the things you can do to help stop acid rain.

Activity 4 **Classifying Birds**

Background Information

Birds are warm-blooded vertebrates that are found in many parts of the world. Although they share many characteristics, such as feathers, wings, and beaks, birds in different environments have their own unique adaptations that enable them to survive. There are more than 8000 species of birds that exist on Earth today. These birds are classified into several general categories. Four of these categories are birds of prey, perching-song birds, wading birds, and waterfowl.

Birds of prey are adapted for hunting. Their broad wings allow them to glide for long distances while they look for prey. They have keen eyesight that enables them to see small animals from great heights. Long, sharp claws on their toes, called talons, hold their prey tightly. Birds of prey also have razor-sharp beaks that can tear small animals into bite-sized pieces.

Perching-song birds are the most common birds. They have claws that allow them to perch, or grasp onto branches and other structures. All perching-song birds make sounds. Some of them make beautiful sounds, while others simply repeat the same sound over and over. Many perching-song birds have beaks adapted for eating seeds and insects. These birds also tend to be small and have short wings.

Wading birds are tall and have long legs, necks, and beaks. Their body structure enables them to feed on animals found in shallow water because they can wade in the water and spear their food with their pointed beaks. The tall bodies of wading birds are supported by toes that can spread wide.

Waterfowl have bodies adapted for life on water. Their broad flat beaks and long flexible necks allow them to reach into the water to find food. With their short, webbed feet they can swim in the same way humans use oars to paddle boats.

Problem

What characteristics are used to classify birds?

Materials

labeled photographs or drawings of the following birds: field sparrow, mallard, great egret, golden eagle, Canada goose, great blue heron, great horned owl, blue jay

Procedure

1. In the appropriate place in Observations, paste the photograph or drawing of each of the eight birds.

2. Classify the birds as one of the following: bird of prey, perching-song bird, wading bird, or waterfowl. Then, write the classification of each bird on the line below its photograph or drawing.

Observations

Field sparrow _____

Mallard _____

Great egret _____

Golden eagle _____

Canada goose _____

Great blue heron _____

Great horned owl _____

Blue jay _____

Analyze and Conclude

1. Which body structures are important in classifying birds?

   _____

   _____

2. Why is it beneficial that perching-song birds are adapted for eating insects and seeds?

   _____

   _____

   _____

3. Wading birds and waterfowl both obtain food in water. Compare the water environments in which these birds are most likely to find food.

   _____

   _____

   _____

4. In what kind of environments are birds of prey able to live? Explain your answer.

   _____

   _____

   _____

5. Many birds migrate, or move to a different environment, during the winter. Why do you think birds migrate?

   _____

   _____

   _____

6. Another group of birds are flightless birds. The emu and the ostrich are examples of flightless birds. What adaptations do you think flightless birds might have for obtaining food?

   _____

   _____

   _____

Name _____ Class _____ Date _____

Activity 1 **Measuring Acceleration**

Background Information

Suppose a car moves northward at 25 km/hr. Its speed is 25 km/hr. Speed is the rate at which an object moves. Its velocity, however, is 25 km/hr north. Velocity is speed in a given direction. If the car were to make a right turn without changing speed, its velocity would be 25 km/hr east.

If the same car were to speed up when it reached a hill, then roll down the other side, making a left turn at the bottom of the hill, it would be experiencing changes in velocity. The rate of change in velocity is known as acceleration. The change in velocity is the difference between the final velocity and the original velocity:

$$\text{Acceleration} = \frac{\text{Final velocity} - \text{Original velocity}}{\text{Time}}$$

If the original velocity of a car is 0 meters per second, and after 10 seconds the velocity increases to 100 meters per second, the velocity changes at a rate of 10 meters/second/second, or 10 m/sec/sec (pronounced meters per second per second). If velocity decreases, the value of acceleration is negative. Negative acceleration is called deceleration.

Roller coasters such as those at Cedar Point in Ohio are thrilling rides because of acceleration and deceleration. During a steep downhill drop, the roller coaster accelerates quickly. By the time it reaches the top of the next hill, it has lost some velocity, or decelerated, only to regain velocity on the next trip downhill.

Problem

How can you measure the acceleration of a roller coaster?

Procedure

1. Study the roller coaster shown in Figure 1 on page 28. At each lettered point on the roller coaster, the distance from the start of the track in meters—and the time it took for the roller coaster to reach that point in seconds—is shown. In the appropriate places in the Data Table, for each point record the distance from the previous point on the track, and the time elapsed since the last point.

2. Calculate the average velocity at each point using the distance from the previous point and the time elapsed since the previous point. Record your calculations in the appropriate places in the Data Table.

3. In the graph provided in Observations, plot the average velocity at each point versus the total time elapsed on the roller coaster ride.

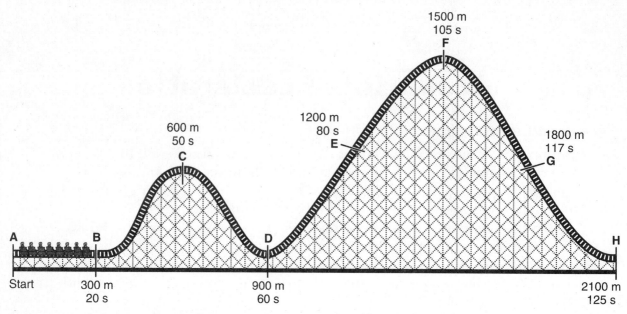

Figure 1

4. Calculate the acceleration at each point using the average velocity at that point as the final velocity, the average velocity at the previous point as the original velocity, and the time elapsed between the two points. Record your calculations in the Data Table.

Observations

DATA TABLE

Point	Distance from previous point	Time elapsed since previous point	Average velocity	Acceleration
A				
B				
C				
D				
E				
F				
G				
H				

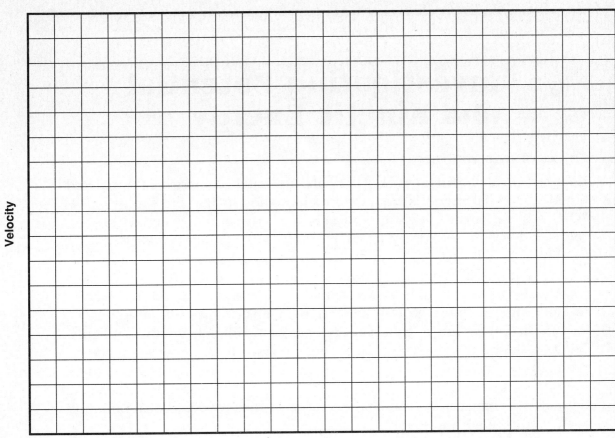

Velocity *(y-axis)*

Time *(x-axis)*

Figure 2

Analyze and Conclude

1. Using the graph in Observations, determine between which sets of two points the roller coaster accelerated. Between which sets of two points did it decelerate?

_____

_____

_____

2. Between which two points was the acceleration fastest? Slowest?

_____

_____

3. Between which two points was the deceleration fastest? Slowest?

_____

_____

Activity 2 Investigating Potential and Kinetic Energy

Background Information

Energy is the ability to do work. There are two states of energy: potential and kinetic. Potential energy is energy stored in matter, such as the energy in fuel. When a fuel is burned, it undergoes a chemical reaction in which energy is released. Food also has potential energy. The energy in food is released when food is broken down by digestion and respiration.

Kinetic energy is energy of motion. Types of kinetic energy are mechanical, electromagnetic, and heat. Mechanical energy is associated with objects in motion, such as a moving car or a falling rock. Electromagnetic energy is energy carried by a moving electric current. It provides electricity that lights buildings and enables electrical appliances to run. Heat energy is the internal motion of atoms, the building blocks of matter. The faster atoms move, the more heat energy they have. Heat energy causes solids to become liquids, and liquids to become gases. Heat energy is used to cook food and heat buildings such as your home and school.

In the International System of Units, abbreviated SI (after the French *Système Internationale d'Unités*), the unit for energy is the joule. A joule is equal to the amount of work done by a force of 1 Newton over a distance of 1 meter. The energy unit used in the United States is the British thermal unit, or Btu. A Btu is the amount of energy required to raise the temperature of 1 pound of water 1° Fahrenheit.

Problem

How does the use of energy sources in different states compare?

Materials (per group)

2 sheets of graph paper

Procedure

1. Study the items pictured in Observations on page 32. Determine which items have kinetic energy and which have potential energy. Then write the word "kinetic" or "potential" inside each box.

2. Data Table 1 lists the potential energy of a variety of fuels. On a sheet of graph paper, construct a bar graph of the data in Data Table 1.

DATA TABLE **1**

Fuel	Potential energy (in megajoules [1 million joules] per kilogram)
Hydrogen	142
Methane	55
Natural gas	52
Gasoline	48
Kerosene	46
Charcoal (pure)	34
Coal	27
Alcohol	27
Wood	13
Dynamite	5

3. Data Table 2 lists the number of Btus of three fuels consumed by the neighboring states of Minnesota and North Dakota during one year. On a second sheet of graph paper, construct a bar graph of this data.

DATA TABLE **2**

Fuel	Amount consumed	
	Minnesota	North Dakota
Petroleum (includes gasoline and kerosene)	616 trillion Btus	118 trillion Btus
Coal	337 trillion Btus	400 trillion Btus
Natural gas	358 trillion Btus	48 trillion Btus

Observations

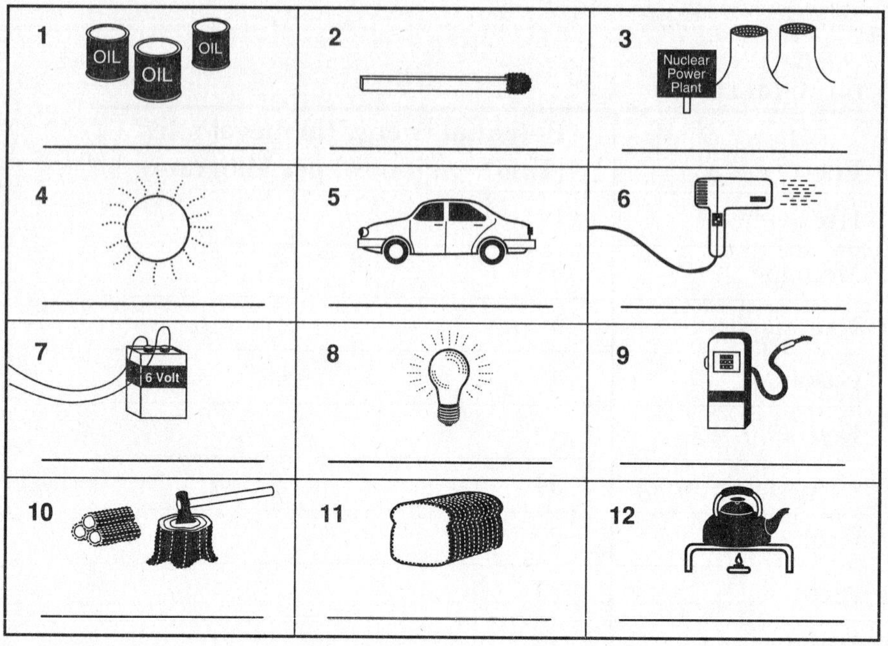

Figure 1

Analyze and Conclude

1. Do the fuels listed in Data Table 1 have potential energy or kinetic energy?

   _____

2. The burning of coal in power plants produces the energy that creates electric currents that go to millions of homes in the United States. Is this electric current an example of potential energy or kinetic energy?

   _____

3. Place the three fuels listed in Data Table 2 in order of increasing potential energy. Which of these fuels is used most in Minnesota? In North Dakota?

   _____

   _____

   _____

4. Do Minnesota and North Dakota use the fuel with the highest potential energy as their main source of energy? If not, explain possible reasons why.

   _____

   _____

   _____

Activity 3 **Determining Wave Speed**

Background Information

A wave is a disturbance that carries energy from one place to another. The matter through which a wave moves is called a medium. One medium through which waves can travel is water. You have probably observed water waves on a lake or at the beach.

The speed of a wave is equal to the frequency of the wave multiplied by the wavelength. The frequency of a wave is the number of complete waves that pass through a given point per unit of time. The wavelength is the distance between two consecutive crests or troughs of a wave. The crest is the highest point of the wave, whereas the trough is the lowest point. See Figure 1. Wave speed is affected by the characteristics of the medium through which the wave travels. One of the factors that affects the speed of a water wave is the depth of the water.

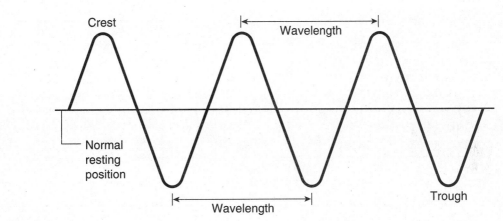

Figure 1

Problem

How does the depth of a body of water affect the speed of waves?

Materials (per group)

two 2-liter plastic bottles with the labels removed
metric ruler
pencil
water

Procedure

1. Label two 2-liter plastic bottles Bottle 1 and Bottle 2.

2. Fill Bottle 1 with water to a depth of 2.5 cm. Fill Bottle 2 with water to a depth of 13 cm. Replace the top on each bottle. Close the bottles tightly.

3. Lay each bottle on its side on a table. Allow the bottles to sit undisturbed until the water stops moving.

4. Measure the height of the water in each bottle from the surface of the table. Record your observations in question 1 of Observations.

5. Lift both bottles 3 cm from the surface of the table at the same time. Gently lower the bottles back to the table. Observe the speed of the waves produced inside each bottle by counting the number of waves that you see in 20 seconds.

6. Allow the bottles to sit undisturbed until the water stops moving. Repeat step 5 three times.

Observations

1. What is the height of the water in each bottle from the surface of the table when the bottles are laid on their side?

_____

_____

2. Compare the speed of the waves produced inside Bottle 1 with the speed of the waves produced inside Bottle 2.

_____

_____

_____

Analyze and Conclude

1. What is the relationship between the depth of the water and the speed of the waves produced?

_____

_____

_____

2. The Great Lakes, located in the midwestern part of the United States, are the largest group of freshwater lakes in the world. The following data table lists the maximum depth of each of the Great Lakes.

DATA TABLE

Great Lake	Maximum Depth
Lake Superior	406 m
Lake Huron	229 m
Lake Erie	174 m
Lake Michigan	281 m
Lake Ontario	244 m

Using the data table on page 34 and your observations, place the lakes in order, from the lake that produces the fastest waves to the lake that produces the slowest waves.

_____

_____

_____

3. Wave speed affects the speed of ships traveling on a body of water. The faster the waves move, the faster a ship traveling in the same direction as the waves will reach its destination. The Great Lakes are important for the shipping industry, especially for the transportation of iron ore and wheat. On which Great Lake do you think the transport of these products is fastest? Slowest?

_____

_____

_____

4. Do you think recreational activities such as fishing, boating, and swimming are influenced by wave speed? Explain your answer. Describe the kinds of recreational activities for which you think the different Great Lakes are most suitable.

_____

_____

_____

_____

_____

_____

_____

_____

_____

_____

Activity 4 **Observing Liquid–Gas Phase Changes**

Background Information

One of the most common physical properties used to describe matter is phase. The three common phases of matter are solid, liquid, and gas. The phase of a substance depends on its energy content. A change in energy content of a substance can be caused by the addition or removal of heat.

When a solid gains enough energy, it changes phase and becomes a liquid. The change of a substance from a solid to a liquid is called melting. When a liquid gains enough energy, it changes phase and becomes a gas. The change of a substance from a liquid to a gas is called vaporization. Vaporization that occurs at the surface of a liquid is called evaporation. When a gas loses enough energy, it changes phase and becomes a liquid. The change of a substance from a gas to a liquid is called condensation.

Problem

How can knowledge of phase changes be used to produce fresh water?

Materials

50 g salt	clear plastic microwaveable container with lid
200 mL water	2 sheets of black construction paper
cup	2 ice cubes
2 straws	desk lamp
metric ruler	

Procedure

1. Combine 50 g of salt and 200 mL of water in a cup. Do not mix the salt and water.

2. After 5 minutes, use a straw to sip a small amount of the mixture from the surface of the water. Drink only enough of the mixture to taste it. **CAUTION:** *Never taste any chemical unless you are instructed to do so.*

3. Add the salt and water to the clear plastic container until it reaches a depth of about 3 centimeters. Put the lid on the container and close it.

4. Fold a sheet of black construction paper in half lengthwise and set it on a flat surface. Carefully move the container onto one half of the construction paper.

5. Place two ice cubes on top of the container lid.

6. Turn on the desk lamp and aim the light toward the bottom of the container

and the construction paper. See Figure 1. The light bulb should be at least 15 cm from the container.

Figure 1

7. Observe the container every 5 minutes for a 30-minute period. Examine the entire container, including the underside of the lid. **CAUTION:** *Be careful when handling the container and lid because they may be hot.* Record your observations in the Data Table.

8. At the end of the 30-minute observation period, carefully open the container. **CAUTION:** *Be careful when handling the container and lid because they may be hot.* Using a clean straw, sip up a small amount of the liquid that has condensed on the bottom of the lid under the ice cubes. Taste the liquid. **CAUTION:** *Never taste any chemical unless you are instructed to do so.*

9. Open the container and allow all the water to evaporate over a period of three days. After three days, place the container on top of the second sheet of black construction paper and examine the inside. Record your observations in the Data Table.

Observations

DATA TABLE

Time (min)	Observations
5	
10	
15	
20	
25	
30	
3 days	

Analyze and Conclude

1. The first time you tasted the water, it was salty. What did the liquid taste like after the 30-minute observation period?

_____

_____

_____

2. Describe what happened to the water on the bottom of the container, in the middle of the container, and on the underside of the lid.

_____

_____

_____

3. When water evaporates, it often leaves some contaminants behind. Describe how you could use a setup similar to the one in the Procedure to produce fresh water.

_____

_____

_____

4. Deep below Detroit, Michigan, are salt mines. One way to mine this salt would be to dissolve it in water and then transfer the mixture to the surface inside a pipe. How could a phase change be used to recover the salt?

_____

_____

_____

5. Many areas of the Midwest have "hard water," which contains many dissolved minerals. These minerals interfere with laundry detergents, form deposits in water pipes, and give the water a bad taste. Describe how you could modify the setup you used in this activity to "soften" hard water.

_____

_____

_____

_____

6. Recently the jet stream drifted south from Canada during the spring, moving cold Canadian air into North Dakota, South Dakota, Minnesota, Wisconsin, and Michigan. When warm, moist air coming from the Gulf of Mexico hit the Canadian air, massive floods resulted in North Dakota, South Dakota, Minnesota, Illinois, Iowa, Missouri, and Ohio. Describe how a phase change is responsible for these floods.

_____

_____

Earth Science Activities

Activity 1 **Locating the Epicenter of an Earthquake**, p. 1

Teacher's Note Provide each group with a photocopy of a map of the United States. Indicate the location of each city whose distance from the epicenter students will measure, or have the students find the locations and mark them on their maps. Make sure the map key includes distances up to 1500 km, with increments of 250 km or less, so that the students will easily be able to set their compasses to the correct radii. Students may need assistance in setting their compasses to the correct radii in order to draw the circles. **Observations Data Table** Distance to epicenter: Indianapolis, IN— 498 km; Wichita, KS—666 km; Bismarck, ND—1548 km; Madison, WI—798 km. **Analyze and Conclude 1.** An S wave takes twice as long as a P wave to reach a seismograph station. **2.** Students' answers may vary according to the accuracy of their measurements and circles. New Madrid, Missouri, is the epicenter; however, you may accept other nearby locations. **3.** Two circles will intersect at two points, giving two possible locations. Three circles, however, will intersect at only one common point. **4.** Check students' drawings for general accuracy. The length of the fault is about 240 km.

Activity 2 **Communicating About the Weather,** p. 4

Teacher's Note Divide the class into five groups. Each group will need a weather report for a different day of a given week. You may obtain the weather reports yourself, or have students obtain them and bring them to class. If you have access to the Internet, you may obtain weather data for cities across the country from the following site: http://www.aws.com/globalwx.html. **Observations Data Table** Sample station model: 3 to 7 knots; southwest; 42°F; 40°F; 985.4 millibars; –20 millibars; 1/2; drizzle; cirrus and altostratus. **Analyze and Conclude 1.** Answers will vary. **2.** Wind direction. **3.** Answers will vary. Students should demonstrate an understanding of the relationships among different weather factors. **4.** The lower the barometric pressure, the greater the amount of clouds. **5.** The lower the barometric pressure, the greater the amount of precipitation. **6.** Station models enable meteorologists to record data and communicate it in a concise way. **7.** Students' predictions may vary; however, they should demonstrate an understanding of weather patterns. **8.** Answers will vary.

Activity 3 **Using a Contour Map to Create a Landform,** p. 8

Teacher's Note Make one enlarged photocopy of the contour map for the Midwest for each group of students. The copy should be approximately the same size as the box lid used in the procedure. **Observations 1.** Answers may vary depending on the accuracy of the landforms, but they should resemble a hill with one steep end and one end with a gentle slope. **2.** 240 meters. **3.** 6 meters. **Analyze and Conclude 1.** Yes. The landforms should resemble a hill with one steep end and one end with a gentle slope. **2.** From the northeast. **3.** Answers may vary. Students might think the hill in the contour map for the Northeast is a drumlin also because one of its ends is steeper than the other. **4.** Answers will vary.

Activity 4 **Observing Erosion and Deposition,** p. 12

Teacher's Note This activity should be done either outdoors or in a location where runoff water can be collected, such as near a large sink. **Observations Data Table** The slope equals elevation of cardboard/length of cardboard. Observations will vary. The water should move faster when the cardboard is raised 15 cm. It should also flow faster and create a wider path when it moves over several rocks than when it moves over one rock. The pile of rocks may cause the water to produce a wider stream. **Analyze and Conclude 1.** The particles were carried to the bottom of the stream or collected on the side. **2.** Smooth curves. **3.** It increased the speed of the water. **4.** The faster the water moved, the more soil it carried and the wider the path of the stream. **5.** The larger the gradient, the faster the rate of erosion. **6.** The water moves faster over the pile of rocks than over a single rock. The gradient of the pile is steeper than the gradient of a single rock. **7.** The boulder causes a change in the direction in which the water moves and increases the speed of the water. **8.** Erosion in the Midwest occurs on a smaller scale than in mountainous regions such as the West.

Life Science Activities
Activity 1 **Investigating Ecological Succession,** p. 15
Teacher's Note Follow these instructions to make the game board and cards: **1.** Using heavy paper, cut out 16 cards of equal size for each pair of students. **2.** Choose two plants and two animals from each community and obtain pictures of them: Open beach—Plants: seaside spurge, cockleburr, bugseed, sea rocket. Animals: spotted sandpiper, tiger beetle, fly, gull. Fore-dune cottonwood—Plants: marram grass, sand thistle, cottonwood, poison ivy, milkweed. Animals: velvet ant, digger wasp, sparrow, snout beetle, lizard. Jack pine—Plants: jack pine, juniper, dogwood, arctic bearberry, dune grass. Animals: black ant, six-line race runner, garter snake, horned owl, chickadee. Oak forest—Plants: witch hazel, basswood, sassafras, Virginia creeper. Animals: raccoon, squirrel, rabbit, deer, cardinal, wood thrush, earthworm. You may want to have students help you find the pictures in books, photocopy them, and glue them to the cards; or have students draw pictures on the cards. The pictures should reflect the relative sizes of the organisms, if possible. **3.** Write the name of the organism on the side of the card on which the picture appears. On the other side of each card, write the name of the community to which the organism belongs, using markers or colored pencils. Write "Open beach" in yellow; "Fore-dune cottonwood" in green; "Jack pine" in red; and "Oak forest" in blue. **4.** To create the game board, arrange the 16 squares in a circle. The squares should be the same size as the game cards. Color four of the squares yellow, the next four green, the next four red, and the last four blue. You might prefer to use construction paper to make the cards and game board.

Analyze and Conclude 1. The open-beach community has the most pioneer plants. Pioneer plants create a layer of soil in which larger plants can grow. **2.** The plants in the oak-forest community are much larger than the plants in the open-beach community. This is because the soil in the oak-forest community contains a lot of humus, which makes it possible for large plants to grow. The open-beach community contains little, if any, humus. **3.** The oak-forest community has mammals. Answers may vary, but students should suggest that mammals require a cool and moist environment and need the food available in the oak-forest community. **4.** Although answers may vary, students should realize that large amounts of sunlight lead to drier conditions, and that only plants and animals adapted to such conditions can survive in such an environment. **5.** The open-beach community was the first to form. The oak-forest community was the last to form. **6.** A heavy storm, a tornado, or a brush fire could disturb the communities.

Such an event could interrupt the process of succession. **7.** Humans have prevented or interrupted succession by activities such as planting farms, constructing buildings and roads, and burning forests. **8.** Answers will vary. If students observe a vacant lot or the bottom of a fence, they may find tall weeds growing. If they observe a wooded area, it might still be in the process of succession, perhaps with only small trees. **9.** Answers may vary; however, students should suggest that the trees in the beech-maple forest are larger than those in the oak forest.

Activity 2 **Classifying Leaves,** p. 18

Observations Students' charts will vary. Check charts for recognition of the characteristics of the leaves. **Analyze and Conclude 1.** Answers will vary. Different classification systems are possible because different students will use different criteria for categorizing the leaves. **2.** Answers will vary. Characteristics that are identical in all leaves, such as color, would not be useful for classifying them. **3.** Terms such as large and small should be avoided because they are relative. There may not be a common standard of size for many organisms. **4.** Classification makes it possible to see relationships among organisms. Organisms that have similar characteristics are closely related. **5.** During winter, one could classify trees using their type of bark, stem, buds, roots, fruit, and growth pattern. Also, conifers can be distinguished from other trees because conifers do not lose their leaves. **6.** Answers will vary.

Activity 3 **Observing the Effects of Acid Rain,** p. 21

Observations 1. North Dakota has a higher pH level. Ohio has a higher acid level. **2.** 3.5. **3.** Minnesota, South Dakota, and Nebraska have national forests in areas where the pH is 5.0 or higher. Missouri and Wisconsin have national forests in areas where the pH is 4.6 to 4.8. **4.** Illinois, Indiana, Michigan, and Ohio. **Analyze and Conclude 1.** These states have the lowest pH because they are closest to major industrial cities. **2.** Minnesota, South Dakota, and Nebraska. **3.** None of the midwestern states has a pH low enough to damage trees and plants. Yes, this could change if acid rain continues to be created. **4.** Answers will vary. **5.** Students may suggest that acid fog is more damaging because it lingers around trees, soaking the leaves in acid precipitation for a longer period of time. **6.** Students should suggest reducing the use of electricity, car-pooling, walking, and using public transportation.

Activity 4 **Classifying Birds,** p. 24

Observations Field sparrow: perching-song; Mallard: waterfowl; Great egret: wading; Golden eagle: bird of prey; Canada goose: waterfowl; Great blue heron: wading; Great horned owl: bird of prey; Blue jay: perching-song. **Analyze and Conclude 1.** Answers may include beak, wings, legs, feet, and feathers. **2.** Because they spend a lot of time in trees, where insects and seeds are abundant. **3.** Wading birds find food in shallow water, such as near beaches or in shallow lakes or ponds. Waterfowl can find food in deep-water environments, such as in deep lakes or the ocean. **4.** Because they have such good eyesight and are able to fly for long periods of time, birds of prey are able to live in many types of environments, including land and water environments. They are probably most successful in areas without a lot of trees, because trees would block their view of food. **5.** Birds migrate to obtain food in warmer climates. **6.** Flightless birds may have such adaptations as long legs to enable them to run to catch prey, long necks to enable them to bend over to catch prey, or webbed feet for swimming to find prey in water.

© Prentice-Hall, Inc.

Physical Science Activities

Activity 1 **Measuring Acceleration,** p. 27

Observations Data Table Point A: 0; 0; 0; 0. Point B: 300 m; 20 s; 15 m/s; 0.75 m/sec/sec. Point C: 300 m; 30 s; 10 m/s; 0.33 m/sec/sec. Point D: 300 m; 10 s; 30 m/s; 3.00 m/sec/sec. Point E: 300 m; 20 s; 15 m/s; 0.75 m/sec/sec. Point F: 300 m; 25 s; 12 m/s; 0.48 m/sec/sec. Point G: 300 m; 12 s; 25 m/s; 2.08 m/sec/sec. Point H: 300 m; 8 s; 37.5 m/s; 4.69 m/sec/sec. Plotted graphs should accurately illustrate changes in velocity over time as recorded in the Data Table. **Analyze and Conclude 1.** The roller coaster accelerated between points A and B, C and D, F and G, and G and H. The roller coaster decelerated between points B and C, D and E, and E and F. **2.** The acceleration was fastest at point H. The acceleration was slowest at point B. **3.** The deceleration was fastest at point E. The deceleration was slowest at point C.

Activity 2 **Investigating Potential and Kinetic Energy,** p. 30

Observations 1. potential **2.** potential **3.** potential **4.** kinetic **5.** kinetic **6.** kinetic **7.** potential **8.** kinetic **9.** potential **10.** potential **11.** potential **12.** kinetic **Graph 1** Students' bar graphs should accurately illustrate the data in Data Table 1. **Graph 2** Students' graphs may vary. Different symbols or shadings can be used to represent the states or fuels. The bar graphs should accurately illustrate the data in Data Table 2. **Analyze and Conclude 1.** Potential energy. **2.** Kinetic energy. **3.** Coal, petroleum, natural gas. Petroleum is used most in Minnesota. Coal is used most in North Dakota. **4.** Neither state uses the fuel with the highest potential energy, natural gas, as their main source of energy. This may be due to an inadequate supply of natural gas, or difficulties in transporting or providing natural gas compared to petroleum or coal.

Activity 3 **Determining Wave Speed,** p. 33

Observations 1. Bottle 1: approximately 1 cm; Bottle 2: approximately 5 cm. **2.** The waves produced inside Bottle 2 move faster than the waves in Bottle 1. **Analyze and Conclude 1.** The deeper the water, the greater the speed of the waves produced. **2.** Lake Superior, Lake Michigan, Lake Ontario, Lake Huron, Lake Erie. **3.** Transport is fastest on Lake Superior and slowest on Lake Erie. **4.** Answers will vary. Students should understand that wave speed can influence recreational activities. For example, fishing would be more difficult on a lake with a faster wave speed because fast-moving waves would prevent the fishing boat from staying in one place. Students should identify the more shallow Great Lakes as those in which recreational activities that require calm water would best be carried out.

Activity 4 **Observing Liquid–Gas Phase Changes,** p. 36

Teacher's Note Use only microwaveable plastic containers for this activity. **Observations Data Table** 5 min.—Slight clouding on sides of container; ice starts to melt; 10 min.—Increased clouding on sides; 15 min.—Condensation of water on underside of lid below ice; 20 min.—Condensation covers half of sides and underside of lid; 25 min.—Condensation covers two-thirds of the sides and lid; 30 min.—Condensation covers underside of lid; some drips down; 3 days—Water has evaporated and salt crystals are left behind. **Analyze and Conclude 1.** After the 30-minute observation period, the liquid should taste "fresh" (not salty). **2.** The liquid water on the bottom of the container gained heat energy from the lamp and air and evaporated at the surface. The air in the middle of the container held increasing amounts of water vapor.

As the water vapor in the air came in contact with the bottom of the cold lid, it gave up energy and condensed into liquid water. **3.** Water containing a contaminant could be evaporated and then condensed and collected in a cold area. **4.** Add heat energy to the saltwater solution in order to evaporate the water and recover the salt. **5.** Answers will vary. Students might suggest transferring the water supply to a heat source to allow evaporation to occur so that minerals are removed before the water reaches its point of use. **6.** When the warm, moist Gulf air hits the cold front, the warm air gives up energy and is cooled. This causes the moisture in the Gulf air to condense and fall as rain. If the ground is saturated and the weather pattern persists, the amount of rain may exceed the capacity of the rivers, causing floods.

Correlation to Prentice Hall Middle Grades Science Programs

The *Student-Centered Science Activities for the Midwest* book is designed to be used with the following Prentice Hall middle grade school science programs:

- *Prentice Hall Exploring Earth Science, Prentice Hall Exploring Life Science,* **and** *Prentice Hall Exploring Physical Science*
- *Prentice Hall Science Explorer*
- *Prentice Hall Science*

Activity	PH Exploring Life, Earth, and Physical Science	PH Science Explorer	PH Science
Earth Science			
1. Locating the Epicenter of an Earthquake	Unit Three: Dynamic Earth Chap. 11: Sec. 11–1	Book F: Inside Earth Chap. 2: Secs. 1 and 2	Book J: Dynamic Earth Chap. 2: Sec. 2–1
2. Communicating About the Weather	Unit Four: Exploring Earth's Weather Chap. 16: Secs. 16–1to16–6	Book I: Weather and Climate Chap. 3: Secs. 1 through 4	Book K: Exploring Earth's Weather Chap. 1: Secs. 1–1 to 1–6
3. Using a Contour Map to Create a Landform	Unit Two: Exploring Planet Earth Chap. 8: Secs. 8–2 to 8–4	Book G: Earth's Changing Surface Chap. 1: Secs. 2, 3, and 5	Book I: Exploring Planet Earth Chap. 4: Secs. 4–2 to 4–4
4. Observing Erosion and Deposition	Unit Three: Dynamic Earth Chap. 15: Sec. 15–4	Book G: Earth's Changing Surface Chap. 3: Sec. 2	Book J: Dynamic Earth Chap. 6: Sec. 6–4
Life Science			
1. Investigating Ecological Succession	Unit Six: Ecology Chap. 27: Sec. 27–3	Book E: Environmental Science Chap. 1: Sec. 4	Book G: Ecology: Earth's Living Resources Chap. 2: Sec. 2–3
2. Classifying Leaves	Unit Two: Monerans, Protists, Fungi, and Plants Chap. 9: Secs. 9–1 and 9–3	Book A: From Bacteria to Plants Chap. 5: Secs. 1 through 3	Book B: Parade of Life: Monerans, Protists, Fungi, and Plants, Chap. 5: Secs. 5–1 and 5–3
3. Observing the Effects of Acid Rain	Unit Six: Ecology Chap. 29: Sec. 29–1	Book E: Environmental Science Chap. 5: Sec. 1	Book G: Ecology: Earth's Living Resources Chap. 4: Sec. 4–1
4. Classifying Birds	Unit Three: Animals Chap. 13: Sec. 13–2	Book A: From Bacteria to Plants Chap. 5: Secs. 2 through 4	Book C: Parade of Life: Animals Chap. 4: Sec. 4–2
Physical Science			
1. Measuring Acceleration	Unit Three: Motion, Forces, and Energy Chap. 12: Sec. 12–3	Book M: Motion, Forces, and Energy Chap. 1: Sec. 4 and Chap. 2: Sec. 2	Book S: Motion, Forces, and Energy Chap. 1: Sec. 1–3
2. Investigating Potential and Kinetic Energy	Unit Three: Motion, Forces, and Energy Chap. 16: Secs. 16–1 to 16–3	Book M: Motion, Forces, and Energy Chap. 5: Secs. 1 and 2	Book S: Motion, Forces, and Energy Chap. 5: Secs. 5–1 to 5–3
3. Determining Wave Speed	Unit Six: Sound and Light Chap. 23: Secs. 23–1 to 23–4	Book O: Sound and Light Chap. 1: Secs. 1 and 2	Book R: Sound and Light Chap. 1: Secs. 1–1 to 1–4
4. Observing Liquid–Gas Phase Changes	Unit One: Matter: Building Block of the Universe Chap. 3: Secs. 3–1 and 3–2	Book K: Chemical Building Blocks Chap. 2: Secs. 1 and 4	Book N: Matter: Building Block of the Universe Chap. 2: Secs. 2–1 and 2–2